CREATE
—IN ME A—
CLEAN HEART

A PASTORAL RESPONSE TO PORNOGRAPHY

A Statement of the
US Catholic Bishops

United States Conference of Catholic Bishops • Washington, DC

The document *Create in Me a Clean Heart: A Pastoral Response to Pornography* was developed by the Committee on Laity, Marriage, Family Life and Youth of the United States Conference of Catholic Bishops (USCCB). It was approved by the full body of the USCCB at its November 2015 General Meeting. It has been authorized for publication by the undersigned.

Msgr. J. Brian Bransfield
General Secretary, USCCB

Scripture texts in this work are taken from the *New American Bible, Revised Edition* © 2010, 1991, 1986, 1970 Confraternity of Christian Doctrine, Washington, DC. and are used by permission of the copyright owner. All rights reserved. No part of the *New American Bible, Revised Edition,* may be reproduced in any form without permission in writing from the copyright owner.

Excerpts from the *Catechism of the Catholic Church, second edition,* copyright © 2000, Libreria Editrice Vaticana–United States Conference of Catholic Bishops, Washington, DC. Used with permission. All rights reserved.

Excerpts from *The Documents of Vatican II*, Walter M. Abbott, SJ, General Editor, copyright © 1966 by America Press, Inc. Reprinted with permission. All rights reserved.

Congregation for Catholic Education, *Educational Guidance in Human Love* © 1983, Libreria Editrice Vaticana (LEV), Vatican City State; Pope Francis, *Laudato Si'* © 2015, Libreria Editrice Vaticana (LEV), Vatican City State; St. John Paul II, *Evangelium Vitae* © 1995, Libreria Editrice Vaticana (LEV), Vatican City State. Used with permission. All rights reserved.

Copyright © 2015, United States Conference of Catholic Bishops, Washington DC. All rights reserved. No part of this work may be reproduced or transmitted in any form or by any means, electronic or mechanical, including photocopying, recording, or by any information storage and retrieval system, without permission in writing from the copyright holder.

ISBN 978-1-60137-527-8

First Printing, December 2015

Contents

I. Introduction 1

II. The Beauty and Vocation of the
    Human Person in Christ 2
    Created in the Image of God and Called to Love 3
    The Gift and Language of the Body 3
    Chastity: A Healthy Vision of Human Sexuality 4
    Sin and Redemption 5

III. Shedding Light on the Sin of Pornography 6
    Defining Pornography 7
    Why Pornography Is an Offense Against
        Chastity and Human Dignity 7
    The Effects of Sin 8
    Pornography's Link to Other Sins 9

IV. The Cultural Pervasiveness of Pornography:
    Landscape and Trends 10
    A Range of Victims 11
    Pervasive Visibility 11
    Acceptability and the Myth of Harmlessness 12
    Technology 12
    An Industry of Sin 13
    Content 13
    Users and Increasing Vulnerability 13

V. A Closer Look at the Effects of Pornography 14
    Men 14
    Women 15
    Addiction 15
    Children and Youth 16
    Marriage and Future Marriages 17
    Parenting and the Family 18

VI. The Church as a "Field Hospital":
    Mercy, Healing, and Hope Through Christ 19
    To Those Exploited by the Pornography Industry 20

    To Those Guilty of Exploiting Others Through the
       Production of Pornography 21
    To Men and Women Who Use Pornography. 21
    To Those Who Have Been Hurt by Their
       Spouse's Pornography Use. 22
    To All Parents. 23
    To All Who Work with Children and Youth. 24
    To Young People. 24
    To Pastors and Other Clergy 25
    To All People of Good Will 26

VII. Conclusion: The Lord Is Rich in Mercy 26
    Prayer 27

Appendix 28
NOTES. 29

I. INTRODUCTION

"A clean heart create for me, God." (Ps 51:12)

As pastors of the Catholic Church, we offer this statement to give a word of hope and healing to those who have been harmed by pornography and to raise awareness of its pervasiveness and harms.[1] In the confessional and in our daily ministry and work with families, we have seen the corrosive damage caused by pornography—children whose innocence is stolen; men and women who feel great guilt and shame for viewing pornography occasionally or habitually; spouses who feel betrayed and traumatized; and men, women and children exploited by the pornography industry. While the production and use of pornography has always been a problem, in recent years its impact has grown exponentially, in large part due to the Internet and mobile technology. Some have even described it as a public health crisis. Everyone, in some way, is affected by increased pornography use in society. We all suffer negative consequences from its distorted view of the human person and sexuality. As bishops, we are called to proclaim anew the abundant mercy and healing of God found in Jesus Christ, our Lord and Savior, and through his Church.

The audience of this statement is broad because pornography affects so many people's lives and requires a collaborative, concentrated effort by all of us to counter its harms. The statement itself is addressed primarily to parents, clergy, diocesan and parish leaders, educators, mental health professionals, and all those in positions to help protect children from pornography and heal the men, women, and young people who have been harmed by its use. We also hope the statement will be helpful for men, women, and young people who themselves view pornography, whether occasionally or habitually, or who have been victimized by pornography. Finally, we speak to religious allies and all people of good will who want to work together toward a culture of purity that upholds the dignity of every person and the sacredness of human sexuality.

The content of the statement is also broad because of the multifaceted nature of this topic. It is structured as follows:

- An overview of the Church's teaching on sexuality, the human person, and chastity
- An explanation of why pornography is sinful and harmful
- A survey of the wide-reaching effects of pornography in our culture
- A closer look at the effects of pornography on men, women, young people, and children
- A word of hope and healing to those harmed by pornography
- An appendix with a link to targeted resources for particular audiences

It is envisioned that further targeted resources will be developed to supplement this statement.

We fervently pray that this statement will contribute to the many good efforts already underway to help men, women, and young people to avoid the sin of pornography and to embrace the freedom and purity of life in Christ. Freedom from pornography is possible! No one needs to fight this battle alone.

II. THE BEAUTY AND VOCATION OF THE HUMAN PERSON IN CHRIST

*"Behold, you desire true sincerity; /
and secretly you teach me wisdom."* (Ps 51:8)

From the beginning of creation, God's beautiful plan for human love was inscribed on the human heart and in the human body. "Male and female he created them" (Gn 1:27). The Church guards, contemplates, and hands on what she has received from Christ. She has the important mission to follow her Lord and, like him, to help the world rediscover God's plan "from the beginning" (see Mt

19:4 and Mk 10:6). The light of Christ illuminates the true beauty and vocation of the human person, and it is a light to be handed on person to person, inviting an encounter with the Lord.[2]

Created in the Image of God and Called to Love

God created the human person, male and female, in his image and likeness, as the crown of creation. Every one of us is a *gift*, with the inviolable dignity of a person. "I praise you, because I am wonderfully made; / wonderful are your works!" (Ps 139:14).

Only in Jesus Christ, true God and true man, is the mystery and identity of the human person fully revealed. "Christ . . . fully reveals man to [man] himself and makes his supreme calling clear."[3] In Christ, we recognize that every person is created to be a *child of God*, a son or daughter in the Son (see Rom 8:14-17). We are each *beloved* by God our Father. This is the Good News!

"God is love" (1 Jn 4:8), the Triune communion of Father, Son, and Holy Spirit.[4] Because each of us is created in the image of God, we are given the call—the vocation—of love and communion.[5] Every human being is made for a relationship of love with God and with others. Jesus, in his life, ministry, and ultimately in his saving Death and Resurrection, shows us the way of love as a sacrificial, fruitful gift of self. Every man and woman, whether called to marriage or not, has a fundamental vocation to self-giving, fruitful love in imitation of the Lord.[6]

The Gift and Language of the Body

Men and women discover the call to love written in their very bodies. The human person is a unity of soul and body, and the body shares in the dignity of the image of God.[7] The body reveals or "expresses the person."[8] It expresses in a visible way one's invisible soul and manifests one's masculine or feminine identity.

St. John Paul II often referred to the "spousal meaning of the body."[9] He taught that the body, in its masculinity or femininity, is inscribed with its own language—a language of gift and of communion of persons. Our bodies tell us that *we come from another*. We are not self-made or fundamentally isolated. Instead, we are each a son or daughter. We are *in relation to* others from the beginning of our existence, first to our mother and father, and through them to the entire human family. Our bodies also tell us that we are "for" another, that we have the capacity for fruitful communion with another, in particular with a person of the opposite sex if called to marriage. Written in our bodies is a call to spousal, fruitful love. This call is realized in marriage as well as in celibacy or virginity for the sake of the Kingdom (e.g., priestly celibacy and consecrated life). In giving ourselves in love, we fulfill the meaning of our existence: "man . . . cannot fully find himself except through a sincere gift of himself."[10]

Because of the beautiful meaning and dignity communicated by our bodies—which communicate our very selves—our bodies should be treated with the greatest respect. We, and therefore our bodies, are not meant to be *used* but *loved*. As Karol Wojtyła (St. John Paul II) taught, the opposite of love is not hate but rather using a person, as if he or she were an object.[11] To love others is to recognize them as the gift they are, to seek what is truly good and best for them, and never to use them and thereby objectify them as something less than persons. The body, then, is not raw, biological matter open to manipulation but is rather inseparable from who we are.[12] As Pope Francis has emphasized, "Learning to accept our body, to care for it and to respect its fullest meaning, is an essential element of any genuine human ecology."[13]

Chastity: A Healthy Vision of Human Sexuality

The virtue and vocation of chastity is essential to love in all its forms.[14] Chastity means "the successful integration of sexuality within the person,"[15] and thus the attainment of self-mastery and genuine freedom in the sexual arena of human action. It is "a virtue that allows us to do what is right, good, and truly loving in the areas of relationship and sexuality."[16] Chastity integrates our internal desires for sexual pleasure into our overall pursuit of moral excellence and holiness. Chastity may be "an unpopular word," but as Pope Francis has indicated, *love is chaste*.[17] "All of us in life have gone through moments in which this virtue has been very difficult, but it is in fact the way of genuine love, of a love that is able to give life, which does not seek to use the other for one's own pleasure."[18]

Chastity is opposed to lust, which is an inordinate desire for sexual pleasure apart from the true meaning of sexuality and marital love.[19] Whereas lust uses another person as a means for sexual gratification, chastity affirms the whole person, body and soul, over and above his or her sexual qualities. It helps us to recognize the great goodness and profound meaning of human sexuality and authentic sexual desire as ordered to the love of man and woman in marriage.[20] The chaste person also seeks to cultivate the virtue of modesty, which inspires one's choice of clothing and behavior out of reverence for the dignity, even mystery, of oneself and others, a reverence which includes appreciation and respect for the human body.[21] While living a chaste life is "a long and exacting work,"[22] it is a path to human flourishing. Chastity calls us to rely on God's grace and to persevere with fortitude in order to resist temptation and make the right decision in challenging circumstances.

All of us are called to live a chaste life. In marriage, chastity takes on the character of permanent, faithful, and fruitful love, and includes the intimate physical, sexual expression of love.[23] The good of sexual pleasure finds its proper place within the embrace of husband and wife. In their wedding vows spoken before God and the Church, a man and a woman freely and without reserve give themselves to each other as husband and wife. Marital love is all-encompassing, a total gift of self, open to new life. As Sacred Scripture attests, this chaste and holy love receives its meaning from and is an analogy for God's faithful, fruitful love (see Eph 5:32).[24]

Sin and Redemption

God created us out of love and for love, but we know that all of history is marked by the sin of our first parents and our own sin.[25] Sin damages our relationships with God, our own selves, others, and all of creation. We are all in need of the Lord's grace, including his mercy and healing.

Sacred Scripture witnesses to the particular harm that sin causes to the relationship between man and woman (see Gn 3:7f.). With Original Sin, the experience of concupiscence (the inclination to sin) entered human history, as well as suffering and death.[26] The original communion of man and woman is now threatened by sin, including the sin of lust.

But we know that sin does not have the last word. Christ has redeemed mankind and has made it possible for us, not only to fulfill God's law, but also to live a new life of freedom in the Holy Spirit. In Jesus, redemption and healing are offered to every person. "Healing the wounds of sin, the Holy Spirit renews us interiorly through a spiritual transformation. He enlightens and strengthens us . . . "[27] The Gospel is indeed very good news.

Our bodies and sexuality are included in Christ's work of redemption, which brings about a new creation that is fulfilled in the glory of the final coming of the Kingdom of God (see Rom 8:18-23). The human body has such great dignity! In the Incarnation, the divine Son assumed a complete human nature, body and soul. By his Resurrection, we look forward to the resurrection of our own bodies. In Baptism, our bodies are made temples of the Holy Spirit (see 1 Cor 6:19). Certainly, none of us is free from weakness and concupiscence, which remain after Baptism. Each of us is caught up in the drama of sin and redemption; we are challenged to put selfishness aside and to strive always toward more perfect love. But the Lord invites us with all our weaknesses to trust and abide in him: "My grace is sufficient for you, for power is made perfect in weakness" (2 Cor 12:9).

III. SHEDDING LIGHT ON THE SIN OF PORNOGRAPHY

"Have mercy on me, God, in accord with your merciful love; / in your abundant compassion blot out my transgressions."
(Ps 51:3)

The Church's teaching on the harm and sinfulness of pornography is grounded in the greater "yes" or affirmation of the inviolable dignity of the human person revealed fully in Christ and the gift of human sexuality and marriage in God's plan. When the Church follows the Lord in upholding the truth of the human person, this involves rejecting anything that would harm that truth. The greater "yes" to the Lord sheds light on the corresponding "no" to the darkness of sin, including injustice. In our duty as pastors and shepherds to proclaim Christ, we must state clearly that all pornography is immoral and harmful and using pornography may lead to other sins, and possibly, even crimes.[28]

Defining Pornography

The *Catechism of the Catholic Church* defines pornography this way:

> Pornography consists in removing real or simulated sexual acts from the intimacy of the partners, in order to display them deliberately to third parties. It offends against chastity because it perverts the conjugal act, the intimate giving of spouses to each other. It does grave injury to the dignity of its participants (actors, vendors, the public), since each one becomes an object of base pleasure and illicit profit for others. It immerses all who are involved in the illusion of a fantasy world.[29]

The moral status of pornography is clear from this passage: producing or using pornography is gravely wrong. It is a grave matter by its object. It is a mortal sin if it is committed with full knowledge and deliberate consent. Unintentional ignorance and factors that compromise the voluntary and free character of the act can diminish a person's moral culpability.[30] This sin needs the Lord's forgiveness and should be confessed within the Sacrament of Penance and Reconciliation. The damage it causes to oneself, one's relationships, society, and the Body of Christ needs healing. Pornography can never be justified and is always wrong.

Pornography does not consist only in visual images (which can be real or virtual, including computer-generated) but can also be in written or audio forms (e.g., certain romance novels, erotic literature, phone conversations, social media, online video chats, etc.). It encompasses what is sometimes distinguished as "soft-" and "hard-core" pornography. This is an artificial divide; all pornography is harmful and wrong, while the effects on a person may vary depending on the intensity of the content. Pornography is not art.[31]

Why Pornography Is an Offense Against Chastity and Human Dignity

Deliberately viewing pornography is a grave *sin against chastity*. Sexual intimacy and the pleasure that derives from it are gifts from God and should remain personal and private, enjoyed within the sacred bond of marriage alone. Such intimacy should not be put on display or be watched by any other person, even if that person is one's own spouse. Nor should the human body be unveiled or treated in a way that objectifies it sexually and reduces it to an erotic stimulant. Jesus is clear in his teaching that sexual immorality is not only a matter of one's actions but also a matter of one's heart: "You have heard that it was said, 'You shall not commit adultery.' But I say to you, everyone who looks at a woman with lust has already committed adultery with her in his heart" (Mt 5:27-28). Regardless of the relationship between the parties, looking at another person with lust—as only a sexual object to enjoy, control, and use—is a sin. It is a *disordered* view of the person, because it is ordered toward *use*, as of a thing, rather than *love*, which pertains to persons. This is why pornography can never be justified, even within marriage.[32]

Pornography is likewise a grave *sin against human dignity*. As the *Catechism* says, filming or taking pictures of the intimate parts of the body or of sexual acts does "grave injury" to the person(s) "performing," to anyone responsible for its making or production, and to the general public.[33] Pornography dehumanizes the persons depicted, making them into objects of use. Those who produce and distribute pornography harm the common good by encouraging and even causing others to sin. They do serious harm to the women and men who consent to be in pornographic material, often out of desperation for money or out of an impoverished sense of self-worth.[34] Even worse, in some cases pornographers take advantage of those who cannot even give consent—children and other victims of human trafficking—which is both a grave sin and a heinous crime.

The Effects of Sin

Sin offends God and always hurts the person sinning as well as the community. To choose with full knowledge and complete consent something gravely contrary to the divine law is to commit a mortal sin,[35] which "destroys in us the charity without which eternal beatitude is impossible."[36] Mortal sin ruptures a person's relationship with God and puts his or her salvation at risk. Forgiveness is needed whenever we sin, and it is always available in the Sacrament of Penance and Reconciliation. Jesus over and over demonstrated his great mercy to sinners, not condemning them but saying, "Go and sin no more" (see Jn 8:1-11). However, persisting in sin can make it more difficult to hear God's call and respond to his offer of mercy, especially if addiction is involved.

Pornography use hurts the user by potentially diminishing his or her capacity for healthy human intimacy and relationships. It presents a distorted view of human sexuality that is contrary to authentic love, and it harms a person's sense of self-worth. Occasional use can turn into more frequent use that can then lead to an addiction to pornography, which is a growing problem, as will be discussed below. Sin also damages the community. It can increase isolation between people because of the feelings of shame and self-reproach it generates. It breaks down trust between family members, and it damages the ability of parents and other adults to be virtuous role models for children.

Pornography's Link to Other Sins

Pornography use is connected with or can lead to other sins in addition to those already mentioned, especially masturbation. Masturbation, which is deliberate, erotic stimulation often to the point of orgasm, commonly occurs together with pornography use. While popular culture largely sees it as acceptable, masturbation is always gravely contrary to chastity and the dignity of one's body.[37] Like other sins against chastity, it seeks sexual pleasure outside of the mutual self-giving and fruitful intimacy of spouses in marriage, in this case, even outside of any relationship at all. In addition, engaging in masturbation has powerful neurological effects that can make it a highly addictive behavior.[38] However, true freedom from this destructive habit is possible with the grace of Christ.

As will be discussed later, pornography use also has direct connections with sins such as adultery, domestic violence, the abuse of children in child pornography, and sex trafficking. It also can be implicated in contraception use and abortion, given that it promotes and even celebrates promiscuity and a view of sexuality devoid of love or openness to new life.

In sum, pornography presents and promotes a distorted view of human sexuality, in which the person portrayed, man or woman, is treated as merely a means of pleasure. Pornography participates in and furthers what Pope Francis has condemned as a "throwaway culture" where things and people are used and discarded.[39] It rejects the equal dignity and complementarity between man and woman and strikes at the heart of God's plan for communion between persons by substituting an image of the viewer's own lustful desires—which is ultimately illusory—for the reality of a true relationship with another human being. Loving, chaste relationships, with all their challenges and struggles, are the only way to true intimacy and community, as well as long-term happiness.

IV. THE CULTURAL PERVASIVENESS OF PORNOGRAPHY: LANDSCAPE AND TRENDS

"For I know my transgressions; / my sin is always before me." (Ps 51:5)

The Church has always had the duty of "scrutinizing the signs of the times" and "interpreting them in the light of the Gospel."[40] Pornography, though not new, is a particularly dark "sign" of the modern world, one that harms countless men, women, children, marriages, and families. Today it can be considered a *structure of sin*.[41] It is so pervasive in sectors of our society that it is difficult to avoid, challenging to remove, and has negative effects that go beyond any one person's actions. At the same time, as with any sin, pornography's prevalence in our society is rooted in the personal sins of individuals who make, disseminate, and view it, and by doing so further perpetuate it as a structure of sin. In the following paragraphs, we as pastors and shepherds evaluate its presence in our society. In imitation of Jesus, the Divine Physician, we examine the sickness of pornography in order to offer a fitting cure: the plentiful mercy and love of God given in the sacraments and in the Church's accompaniment of those who strive steadfastly toward purity.

A Range of Victims

There are many victims of pornography. Every person portrayed in it is beloved by God our Father and is someone's daughter or son. Their dignity is abused as they are used for others' pleasure and profit. Pornography has connections to sex trafficking and commercial sexual exploitation worldwide,[42] an evil that we, as bishops, have condemned strenuously.[43] Many sex-trafficking victims (mostly women and girls) are forced into prostitution, which may include pornography as "training" or as their "product."[44] All child pornography is automatically trafficking and a crime, because it involves the sexual exploitation of a minor for commercial gain and it is against the child's will due to the inability to give consent.[45] The actors in pornographic films also face serious risks, such as contracting a sexually transmitted infection (STI) and high rates of drug and alcohol abuse.[46]

There are also collateral effects from pornography use everywhere in the culture. Viewing pornography conditions men (and women) to look at other human beings simply as sexual objects,[47] rather than as persons who deserve respect and love. They are trained in a "pornographic gaze" and "habit of objectification."[48] Women in particular may begin to see and present themselves as sexual objects, dressing or acting in a sexual manner, even at a young age,[49] and pursuing an idealized, falsified image of female beauty that can lead to mistreatment of their bodies, including eating disorders. Women (and men) may feel pressured to engage in degrading sexual acts that are portrayed in pornography.[50] There is also more serious collateral damage in terms of violence against women. Much of pornography is violent,[51] and when for example men view it, they are more likely to sexually abuse a girlfriend or wife.[52]

Pervasive Visibility

Erotic, over-sexualized, and pornographic images are more present in American society than ever before. It is commonplace to see these images while reading magazines and social media content, shopping online or at the mall, or watching movies and television. Mainstream entertainment itself has become hypersexualized. Novels that at one time would have been classified as "erotica" are now mainstream, to say nothing of the overtly sexual romance novel genre. Video games, music lyrics, music videos, clothing, and even costumes have become progressively more sexualized, including content targeted to children and adolescents.[53] Maintaining purity is a serious challenge in this environment, as is learning appropriate boundaries that are necessary for living chastely and having healthy relationships.

Acceptability and the Myth of Harmlessness

Pornography is often misrepresented as a harmless pastime (using euphemisms like "adult entertainment" or "gentlemen's club") or even promoted as good—for example, as an aid to marital intimacy. It is not uncommon to hear pornography use described as "normal" for men, implying that they are "hard-wired" to look at it. Many people, more men than women, do not consider viewing pornography to be cheating, that is, being unfaithful to one's spouse or girlfriend/boyfriend.[54] Pornography also desensitizes its viewers, who may seek out and watch more extreme and degrading content over time as their tolerance increases.[55]

Technology

The rise of the Internet presents the most dramatic difference between pornography in decades past and more recently. While online media can be a fruitful avenue for evangelization and personal encounter,[56] the Internet also runs the risk of appealing to a desire for instant gratification and replacing human presence with "virtual reality." Online, pornography is instantly accessible, seemingly anonymous, mostly free, and has the appearance of being endlessly novel. This potent combination has had devastating effects on many men and women. The widespread availability of the Internet means that pornography is in the home, at work, and often literally at one's fingertips with the prevalence of mobile devices. The Internet's perceived anonymity can entice a person to view images or engage in activities that he or she would hesitate to do off-line, and the novelty of Internet pornography can itself be intoxicating, affecting brain chemistry and seducing viewers to keep clicking.[57] In contrast to a magazine, the Internet has no final page.

An Industry of Sin

Pornography is a big business. Estimates of revenue stretch easily into the billions of dollars every year.[58] The pornography industry is aggressive, savvy, and regulated only sporadically, even though child pornography or content that is considered "obscene" is illegal to make, sell, own, or view.[59] Many companies invest heavily in lobbyists to push "free speech" ordinances to counter legal charges of indecency and obscenity.[60] Pornographers often use free online content as bait to entrap and addict new users who will then pay to access "exclusive" material. Marketers target young men especially with sexual ads on popular sports and social media websites. Other businesses, such as hotel chains, cable companies, and drugstores, profit greatly from the widespread use of pornography and contribute to its accessibility. The pornography industry and its pervasive reach is a clear sign that pornography has become a structure of sin in our society.

Content

All pornography exploits both the persons portrayed and the viewer and is devoid of love and relationship. But the kinds of content available today are becoming increasingly coarse, violent, degrading, and even satanic with overt portrayals of occult practices. A majority of pornographic scenes include physical or verbal aggression and violence, communicating the message that sex is abusive, rough, and degrading.[61] Many scenes also include sexual activity between persons of the same sex, portrayals that are viewed by persons regardless of their real-life attractions. Pornographic scenes usually involve real people, but they can also be computer-generated.

Users and Increasing Vulnerability

Given how widespread and easily accessible pornography is in today's society, everyone is vulnerable. Many people struggle with pornography use, including faithful Catholics, people of faith, people of no faith, married and single people, fathers and mothers, the young and the old, clergy and those in consecrated life.[62] Some people have only seen pornography a handful of times, perhaps unintentionally; some view it occasionally; while others find themselves compulsively viewing pornography, perhaps despite their best intentions to resist. While more men than women use pornography, the number of women users is growing.[63] Pornography use is especially high among young adults,[64] and it has been reported that the average age of first exposure to pornography is as early as eleven, with boys being more likely than girls to be exposed at an earlier age and to view more extreme content before the age of eighteen.[65]

V. A CLOSER LOOK AT THE EFFECTS OF PORNOGRAPHY

"Thoroughly wash away my guilt; / and from my sin cleanse me." (Ps 51:4)

All men and women are created in the image of God and are called to love God and others. Pornography use damages the ability of men and women to become who they are called to be. It makes it more difficult for them to be in self-giving, mutually respectful relationships with each other. It attacks a man's call to love and protect women and to sacrifice for them, and it undermines a woman's capacity to love and cherish another human being as a gift and to be received as a gift. Here, we take a closer look at the costly toll of pornography on men, women, young people and children, with a special emphasis on marriage and family life.

Men

Men are particularly susceptible to pornography because the male brain is strongly drawn to sexual images, a kind of "visual magnetism"[66] aggressively exploited by the pornography industry. There are a variety of reasons why a man might view pornography, from "recreation" to seeking comfort for emotional wounds (e.g., low self-esteem, feeling unlovable)[67] to a desire for a sense of power. The effects of pornography on those who view it are becoming better documented and more understood. They include physiological, financial, emotional, mental,[68] and spiritual effects (see below for more information). Those who use pornography can often experience a deep sense of shame and an erosion of self-worth. Men in particular can develop a narcissistic self-identity[69] and an inflated sense of "machismo." Viewing pornography can distort one's view of sexuality, marriage,[70] and the opposite sex, and can cause confusion about one's own sexual identity and inclinations (a confusion exacerbated by viewing same-sex pornography). Spiritually, like any sin, using pornography damages one's relationship with God. Users often believe falsely that God could never love them, and they may despair of his mercy and healing.

Women

Pornography is not just a men's issue. Women use pornography for similar reasons as men and experience similar effects.[71] While it is not uncommon for women to view compulsively the same extreme visual content as men, they have traditionally tended to gravitate toward forms of pornography that promise relational connection and romance, such as erotic literature or inappropriate social media interactions and video chats.[72] Women face the added challenges of the faulty assertion that using pornography is liberating for them, and the false societal perception that only men use pornography or struggle with pornography addiction, which can cause a deep sense of shame and isolation.

Addiction

Both science and personal testimonies confirm that many people who start by occasionally viewing pornography later become compulsive viewers who feel trapped in a cycle of fantasy, ritual, acting out, and despair.[73] Viewing pornography, usually combined with masturbation, directly affects the brain's reward pathways and has been noted to have a similar effect on the brain as cocaine does on a person with a drug addiction or as alcohol on a person with an alcohol addiction.[74] After using pornography, the person craves more and over time seeks out a higher number of and/or more extreme images to get the same "high." A person addicted to pornography may become obsessed with viewing pornography, may take increased risks to view it (such as accessing it at work), may continue viewing it despite adverse consequences to self and others, and may feel out of control or helpless to stop.[75] He or she may also deny that a problem exists. While pornography addiction can happen via free online content, compulsive pornography users may spend large amounts of money on "exclusive" online content, go to strip clubs, or solicit prostitution.[76] The moral culpability of an addicted person may be lessened depending on the circumstances, but the situation is particularly grave.[77] Addictions are very hard to overcome, and help is needed to regain one's freedom. We invite the many good men and women who suffer from addiction to pornography to trust in the Lord's mercy and seek appropriate help, support, and resources (see Appendix).

Children and Youth

Young people born in the digital age have grown up immersed in media and the Internet, and many times are savvier at navigating this world than their parents.[78] Since it is estimated that the average age of first exposure to pornography is eleven,[79] many children exposed to pornography are even younger. Almost all young males and over half of young females see pornography before age eighteen, often accidentally, such as finding a family member's "stash" or happening upon a pornographic website through a pop-up ad or typo.[80] Other times a child may search online for a term he or she heard and did not understand, or intentionally search for online pornography out of curiosity. Sex education curriculums may treat pornography as neutral or even good, in some cases even using it as a "teaching tool."[81] Children and teens experience pressure from peers and even family members to look at pornography. More and more, young people produce their own pornography, in the form of sexual photographs or videos shared with peers.[82] "Sexting" is associated with other risky sexual behaviors,[83] charges of child pornography,[84] and tragically has even led to suicide when the image is shared with unintended recipients.[85]

Being exposed to pornography can be traumatic for children and youth. Seeing it steals their innocence and gives them a distorted image of sexuality, relationships, and men and women, which may then affect their behavior. It can also make them more vulnerable to being sexually abused, since their understanding of appropriate behavior can be damaged.[86] A child who is exposed to pornography may experience a mixture of pleasure, pain, disgust, guilt, and curiosity. Without a trusted parent or other adult with whom to talk through these feelings, a child may disengage from family relationships and return to viewing pornography to try to understand his or her feelings. Children and teens who view pornography in effect receive an education about sexuality from what they are viewing. They are more likely to be more accepting of premarital sex,[87] to view women as sex objects,[88] and to overestimate the prevalence of certain degrading sexual practices.[89] They also tend to engage in sexual activity earlier than their peers[90] and are more likely to participate in risky sexual behavior,[91] which puts them at greater risk of getting pregnant as a teenager (or impregnating someone) or contracting an STI. They are at increased risk of sexual addiction later in life.[92] For girls, an over-sexualized society in general and pornography in particular can contribute to low self-esteem, eating disorders, and depression.[93] Data indicates that children repeatedly exposed to pornography are more likely to sexually harass or molest other children, imitating the behavior they have seen.[94]

Tragically, children and youth are also victimized by being forced or coerced into participating in the production of child pornography. Child pornography is illegal,[95] abusive, and a form of human trafficking because of a child's inability to consent.[96] There are many reasons why a child might become a victim of child pornography, including extreme poverty, deplorable neglect by his or her parents or guardians, or manipulation by child pornographers.[97] Children and youth exploited in this way face serious side effects and need plentiful resources for emotional, psychological, and physical healing. Most of all, they need to know that the abuse was not their fault or choice, no matter how their abusers deceived them.

Marriage and Future Marriages

Using or creating pornography within marriage is always wrong and can never be justified.[98] It violates marital chastity and the dignity of the spouses. Pornography use within marriage severely damages the spouses' trust and intimacy both because of the pornography use itself and because of the deception and lies usually involved in one spouse hiding his or her behavior from the other. It has been identified by divorce lawyers as a major factor in over half of divorces.[99] Spouses who discover their husband's or wife's pornography use will often feel betrayed, and many experience a sense of trauma akin to post-traumatic stress disorder.[100] Data also indicates that husbands and wives who use pornography are more likely to have an extramarital affair.[101] Contrary to the common idea that pornography can be an aid to marital intimacy, pornography use tends to decrease sexual satisfaction and interest in sex[102] and can lead to impotence in men.[103] One spouse might also feel degraded by the other's requests for demeaning forms of sexual activity common in pornography.[104] In contrast, God's plan for marriage and chastity within marriage brings real happiness and intimacy to couples; the Church wants this for all husbands and wives!

For single men and women, viewing pornography can make it more difficult to discern and embrace a vocation, whether to marriage, priesthood, or consecrated life. It can damage the ability to enter and maintain a self-giving relationship of mutual trust and respect, in part because it trains viewers to use another person for their own physical pleasure. Pornography increases isolation and can discourage young adults from undertaking the work of a relationship in the first place, because it promises "satisfaction" from an undemanding source.[105] Undoubtedly, pornography fuels the hook-up culture by promoting sexual encounters without relationship.[106] A young man must take risks to win the heart of a woman; he faces no such risks by viewing images on the computer. Because of the shame and feelings of unworthiness that come with pornography use, some young adults may not feel they "deserve" a real, healthy relationship.

Parenting and the Family

In his 2014 Lenten message, Pope Francis noted, "How much pain is caused in families because one of their members—often a young person—is in thrall to alcohol, drugs, gambling or pornography!"[107] Parents today face increasing challenges in protecting their children's innocence. Pornography can enter the home through a variety of doors. The most obvious is media and technology, which includes not only computers, tablets, and mobile phones but also video games connected to the Internet. Many parents feel ill-equipped to understand the various devices their children use, let alone monitor them or install parental controls or filters. Another challenge parents face is the occasion of events such as campouts or sleepovers, where children could be exposed to pornography by peers or even other adults, while their parents are not present.

The use of pornography by anyone in the home deprives the home of its role as a safe haven and has negative effects throughout a family's life and across generations. Parents struggling with pornography addiction waste time watching pornography, and they may inflict financial burdens on the family through their compulsion. Fatherhood is gravely impacted because a son will look to his father as a model, and a daughter will look to her father to understand how a man should treat a woman. Lastly, given pornography's strong correlation with divorce, many children suffer the effects of their parents' divorce as "collateral damage" to pornography use.

VI. THE CHURCH AS A "FIELD HOSPITAL": MERCY, HEALING, AND HOPE THROUGH CHRIST

"Cleanse me . . . that I may be pure; / wash me, and I will be whiter than snow." (Ps 51:9)

Pope Francis reminded the Church of her calling to become a "field hospital" for the wounded of the world.[108] All of us are wounded, starting with Original Sin and its consequences as well as our own sins. In the wake of the so-called sexual revolution, many have been hurt by their own sins, the sins of others, confusion, and broken relationships and families. In particular, the effects of pornography on the soul can be deep, and the use of pornography itself can be a sign of other emotional wounds. No wound is so deep, however, as to be out of the reach of Christ's redeeming grace.

The Church as a field hospital is called to proclaim the truth of the human person in love, to protect people—especially children—from pornography, and to provide the Lord's mercy and healing for those wounded by pornography. Many means of support are available for those who have been harmed by pornography and who desire to be free from it and its effects.

Christ is our hope! Through the outpouring of the Holy Spirit and the mission of his Church, Jesus continues to give us himself, so that we can follow and abide in him. We encounter him in multiple ways: through Sacred Scripture, the sacraments, and the whole teaching and life of the Church. Jesus is the way of freedom. The Church says, "Be not afraid!" Come to the Lord Jesus, whose mercy endures forever! The Lord never tires of forgiving.[109]

With the mercy of God in mind, we now wish to turn here and apply this measure of hope to the concrete circumstances faced by members of the Body of Christ and all people. As bishops responsible for the pastoral care of those who have been or could be affected by pornography, we wish to specifically address Catholics in a range of circumstances and present opportunities for guidance, healing, and grace. In doing this, we are mindful of the particular importance of Catholic leaders and parents who can implement the Church's vision and outreach and be conduits of the Lord's mercy and truth in direct and powerful ways by their witness and service.

To Those Exploited by the Pornography Industry

You are beloved and cherished by God! The Church reaches out to you, especially those victimized by sex trafficking and commercial sexual exploitation and all children who have been involved in the making of child pornography and thereby victimized and abused. The way you have been treated is deplorable and gravely unjust, and we will continue to work for justice and freedom for all enslaved men, women, and children. No matter what you have experienced in your past, remember that you remain beloved by God, have inviolable dignity, and are worthy of respect and love. Come to the Lord through his Church to receive his care for you. Allow him to bind your wounds and give you his strength. Know that there are support groups and resources available to help you (see Appendix). To anyone who has been criminally exploited, we urge immediate reporting to the proper civil authorities and appropriate action to ensure your safety and protection.

To Those Guilty of Exploiting Others Through the Production of Pornography

The Lord, in his great mercy and justice, is calling you to turn away from your sins and follow him. Christ is passing by: do not wait to change your life. Come down, like Zacchaeus, and make amends for the damage you have done (see Lk 19:1-10). No sin is too great to forgive, but we exhort you to repent, convert and put an end to your involvement in spreading the destructiveness of pornography. If you are also (or have been) engaged in criminal exploitation, we urge you to report your action and to hand yourself over to civil authorities. God can use your previous mistakes to help others. Jesus called St. Paul, the "foremost of sinners," to be an Apostle; may he also free and heal you (see 1 Tim 1:15).

To Men and Women Who Use Pornography

You are beloved sons and daughters of the Father. *Be not afraid* to approach the altar of mercy and ask for forgiveness. Many good people struggle with this sin. You are not alone; there is always hope! Satan, the father of lies, uses shame and fear to keep souls from Jesus' mercy, but God, the most loving of Fathers, is waiting to meet with joy those who repent and to give them the grace they need to combat future temptation. Receive the sacraments regularly to gain God's help in your trials, especially the Sacrament of Penance and Reconciliation, through which the Lord forgives a person of mortal sin so that he or she can receive the Sacrament of the Eucharist worthily. Do not let the obstacles of denial, shame, fear, despair, or pride keep you from relying on the Lord's grace. Believe in the power of God. Ask the Holy Spirit for grace and strength. Trust in Jesus' mercy. Ask for the intercessory prayer support of the saints in Heaven.

Knowing the truth of who you are in God and receiving spiritual help are critical, but those who use pornography often need further assistance. Freedom from pornography is a daily choice and calls for ongoing formation. The Church encourages you to seek ongoing support such as counseling, spiritual direction, coaching, accountability groups, couple to couple groups, conferences, and retreats for men and women. These are all means to employ as you seek freedom (see Appendix). Software is available for monitoring online activity and blocking pornographic material; these may be a necessary means of avoiding the near occasion of sin. If your pornography use has become an addiction, it is even more crucial that you have accountability and the support of professionals who can assist in identifying and healing any emotional wounds that may lie at the root of pornography use. For husbands and wives, counseling professionals can help you disclose to your spouse the struggle you face with pornography in a way that leads to healing and the rebuilding of trust. It is important to find a counselor who will support you in following the Church's teachings on marriage and chastity.

Cultivating chastity takes work, as does any growth in virtue. It is a lifelong task and a daily choice. Be patient, persevere, and do not be discouraged. If you fall, get up again, go to the Lord in confession and seek his mercy in the Sacrament of Penance and Reconciliation, and start anew. There is no shame in confessing repeated sins of this kind. Once you are free, helping others find their way out of pornography use can be an effective way of staying committed and strong in your own healing. God can use your experience to touch the hearts and lives of others who are struggling.

To Those Who Have Been Hurt by Their Spouse's Pornography Use

You are greatly loved by God our Father! You are not alone, nor are you to blame for your spouse's pornography use. The Church accompanies you with love and tenderness as you confront this sin and its effects on your marriage and family life. You have been deeply hurt. You feel betrayed, deceived, and even traumatized at finding out about your spouse's pornography use through their own disclosure or your discovery. You may have faced abuse or violence. If you are in a dangerous environment, remove yourself and your children from any danger and seek help.[110] Christ can ultimately heal these wounds, and often it takes time. Seek solace in prayer, in receiving the sacraments, and in eucharistic adoration. Anger at your spouse is natural and often justified, and it can be helpful to have a spiritual director or trained, trustworthy counselor to help you work through powerful emotions.

God wants to heal your marriage.[111] For some of you, your spouse may want to seek help. The encouragement, unconditional love, and trusting hope of a spouse can be a great source of strength for someone who is struggling to be pure. For those of you whose spouse is in denial or rejects help, know that the Church is here for you. Pray for your spouse's change of heart and seek opportunities to encourage him or her. Set clear boundaries if possible, such as installing an online monitoring program, clearing the home of any pornography, taking care of your own health, and refusing to be used as an excuse for your spouse's pornography use. There are support groups and counselors for spouses of addicted persons that can help you in this struggle (see Appendix). Remember, you are not alone! The Church wants to help and encourage you and asks those brave enough to acknowledge their own experience with this issue to help other hurting spouses in the community.

To All Parents

Thank you for your great love and sacrifice! You are cherished by God the Father, from whom your fatherhood and motherhood is named. You are the first guardians and teachers of your children and are called to be their models of chaste and fruitful love. The Church is so grateful for you who form, protect, and guide the domestic Church. As they grow up, children secure in their parents' love for each other and for them will have a distinct advantage in navigating the challenges of the world. Children have the right to receive "an authentic education in sexuality and in love," which includes education in chastity.[112] It is your great and crucial responsibility to teach your children the true meaning of human sexuality, enabling them to see its beauty as an expression of total love. Even from an early age, your children can learn self-control, modesty, and respect for others from your words and actions. Education in chastity also includes doing whatever you can to protect your children from pornography and helping them to reject it and other sexual sins as they mature. There are good resources to help you in this important task (see Appendix).

Parents and guardians, protect your home! Be vigilant about the technology you allow into your home and be sensitive to the prevalence of sexual content in even mainstream television and film and the ease by which it comes through the Internet and mobile devices. Educate yourselves about filtering software that can assist in protecting your home. Foster openness and trust with your children, so they know that they can come to you if they see a sexual image; by talking about it with them calmly, you can give them a healthy framework in which to interpret it. The Holy Spirit is your guide as you assess the situation of each child. None of us is perfect, and parents are the first to model the mercy and forgiveness that all families need. Rely on the Father's mercy, especially if you face the difficult situation of a child who has seen or uses pornography. Many good families experience this; you are not alone, and the Church is here for you.

To All Who Work with Children and Youth

Grandparents, godparents, teachers, religious educators, youth ministers, and safe environment coordinators: parents have given you a responsibility to protect their children not only from physical dangers but also psychological, moral, and spiritual dangers. You can have a great influence on the children and youth entrusted to your care, and you can help equip parents with the resources they need to protect and teach their children. Children are vulnerable to all influences, good or bad. Create an environment suitable for learning chastity by modeling and teaching the chaste life. Be vigilant over technological access, and monitor it in age-appropriate ways. Young people should be taught that certain types of websites or programs are inappropriate and sinful. Be sure to explain the reasons why they are unacceptable.

To Young People

You are loved and cherished by God and called to greatness! Christ calls you to be strong, courageous witnesses of chastity and hope. Adolescence and young adulthood can be a difficult and confusing time, and the desire for sexual intimacy can be strong. Show your friends and peers that chastity brings freedom and joy! It also lays the foundation for a happy, lasting marriage. Reject the lies of a culture that tells you that self-gratification is the road to happiness. Reject pressure to treat sexual activity as recreational. Refuse to objectify your body or someone else's through sexual pictures or videos. God created you in his image, and the Church looks at you with compassion and love, no matter what others may think or say or do. Even more, your body is a temple of the Holy Spirit, and you were made for greatness. If you have already engaged in pornography use, choose now to turn away from that road and toward true relationships, and seek the Lord's forgiveness in the Sacrament of Reconciliation. Jesus loves you and gave his life for you. Do not be afraid to ask for help or guidance from your mother and father or from a trusted adult, family member, or pastoral minister, if you have grown up in an environment where pornography use regularly occurred, or if you were exposed to it at an early age.

To Pastors and Other Clergy

We are witnesses of the joy and freedom of chastity. Our example of chastity as ordained ministers, complemented by others' chastity in marriage, consecrated life, or as single persons helps show the world that it is possible to persevere in virtue with the help of Christ and that it is a gift, not a burden. Recognizing the harm caused by the sin of pornography, let us call the faithful to the Sacrament of Reconciliation often, making sure that it is clearly and readily available. We are aware, too, that clergy and our brothers and sisters in religious communities struggle in this area. Let us approach the fount of mercy ourselves, knowing that we are in need of the Lord's help to live a consistent witness of chastity. Let us be emboldened to preach on chastity, looking to Christ himself, and call attention to the harm of pornography in appropriate ways. We must see our role in protecting children from pornography as our sacred duty, as well as an aspect of our work to create safe environments in accord with our ongoing implementation of the *Charter for the Protection of Children and Young People*.[113] May we educate ourselves on reliable resources for pastoral support of the faithful and for the healing of pornography use and addiction and make them available to families, parishioners, and others in our care. We should also find and promote trustworthy counselors and support groups in our local areas to whom we can refer men and women for help and healing.

Above all, let us live in our own lives the witness of a joyful and pure heart. The importance of seminary formation and ongoing priestly formation, in addition to formation for permanent deacons, is critical, as are regular confession, spiritual direction, fraternal support, and developing authentic friendships. Such ongoing formation and support are vital for all those in consecrated life as well. We must not isolate ourselves. If any of us or our brother clergy is struggling with pornography, may we not be afraid to acknowledge this and to seek help immediately.

To All People of Good Will

The Church advocates for a culture in which purity, chastity, and authentic love are esteemed and supported and pornography is resisted and rejected. The Church is grateful to all who are working to acknowledge the harmful and destructive nature of pornography and speaking up against its proliferation. May we work together for laws and for a culture that remove pornography from its prominent and privileged place and counter its numerous injustices, building instead a culture that honors the true dignity and meaning of human sexuality.

VII. CONCLUSION: THE LORD IS RICH IN MERCY

"You will let me hear gladness and joy." (Ps 51:10)

As we close, we assure all who are struggling with the sin of pornography and striving to cultivate chastity that you are not alone in your struggle. Jesus is with you, and the Church offers you love and support. Trust in and be led by the Holy Spirit. The Lord's mercy and forgiveness are abundant! "As far as the east is from the west, / so far has he removed our sins from us" (Ps 103:12). God's grace and concrete help are always available. Healing is always possible. We thank all men, women, and young people who are helping to build a culture of authentic love and chastity and helping others live a life of freedom and purity.

The Church also looks to the saints. Their example and intercession are a great help for us. In a particular way, we invite renewed devotion to the Holy Family and entrustment to the Immaculate Heart of Mary and Sacred Heart of Jesus. Like many of us, Jesus, Mary, and Joseph experienced the joys and struggles of everyday family life—and they did it with great love and purity. At the center of their chaste love was Jesus Christ, and in this way their love serves as a model for all. Jesus is meant to be at the center of our love and relationships as well. Joseph was a righteous man and is a powerful intercessor for all struggling to be pure, especially men. Mary's Immaculate Heart and Jesus' Sacred Heart unveil the purity and freedom intended for the heart of every woman and man.

Prayer

Have mercy on me, God, in accord with your merciful love;
   in your abundant compassion blot out my transgressions.
Thoroughly wash away my guilt;
   and from my sin cleanse me.
For I know my transgressions;
   my sin is always before me.
Against you, you alone have I sinned;
   I have done what is evil in your eyes
So that you are just in your word,
   and without reproach in your judgment.
Behold, I was born in guilt,
   in sin my mother conceived me.
Behold, you desire true sincerity;
   and secretly you teach me wisdom.
Cleanse me with hyssop, that I may be pure;
   wash me, and I will be whiter than snow.
You will let me hear gladness and joy;
   the bones you have crushed will rejoice.
Turn away your face from my sins;
   blot out all my iniquities.
A clean heart create for me, God;
   renew within me a steadfast spirit.

(Ps 51:3-12)

APPENDIX

The Catholic Church and many other communities and organizations are committed to providing men, women, parents, and leaders with the tools they need to find freedom from pornography and help others do the same. Please visit the USCCB-run webpage ***www.usccb.org/cleanheart*** for an updated selection of resources related to this statement. In general, we encourage evaluation of all resources and programs to determine whether in their teaching and practice Catholic principles are upheld. The webpage content includes the following type of resources:

- List of support groups and recovery programs for those who have been affected by pornography: men and women who use or are addicted to pornography and their spouses and family members; men and women involved in the pornography industry; and others
- Advice and resources for parents, grandparents, and all who work with children and young people and wish to protect their innocence
- Preaching resources for priests and deacons
- Internet filtering tools to block pornographic content on computers and all devices connected to the Internet
- Educational resources with additional information about the harms of pornography
- Other Catholic statements about pornography . . . and more

NOTES

Note: Various references are cited in this statement, including scientific studies, media articles, and books meant for a popular audience. Their inclusion does not imply endorsement of an author or his or her work, or agreement with an author's position on pornography or other moral issues, but is used for illustration of the points in the statement.

1. See *Catechism of the Catholic Church* (2nd ed.) (CCC) (Washington, DC: Libreria Editrice Vaticana [LEV]–United States Conference of Catholic Bishops [USCCB], 2000), no. 2354. For other examples of recent teaching, see also St. John Paul II, Address to the Members of the Religious Alliance Against Pornography (January 30, 1992); Pontifical Council for Social Communications, *Pornography and Violence in the Communications Media: A Pastoral Response* (May 7, 1989); United States Catholic Conference, Statement *Renewing the Mind of the Media* (1998); USCCB, *Catechetical Formation in Chaste Living: Guidelines for Curriculum Design and Publication* (2008), especially 11; USCCB, Pastoral Letter *Marriage: Love and Life in the Divine Plan* (2009), especially 49; and Bishop Paul S. Loverde, Pastoral Letter *Bought with a Price*, new ed. (March 19, 2014).
2. See Pope Francis, Encyclical Letter *Lumen Fidei* (Washington, DC: USCCB, 2013), no. 37; Apostolic Exhortation *Evangelii Gaudium* (Washington, DC: USCCB, 2013), no. 3.
3. Second Vatican Council, Pastoral Constitution *Gaudium et Spes* (Dec. 7, 1965), no. 22, in *The Documents of Vatican II*, ed. Walter M. Abbott (New York: Guild Press, 1966).
4. See CCC, nos. 261-263.
5. See St. John Paul II, Apostolic Exhortation *Familiaris Consortio* (Washington, DC: USCCB, 1982), no. 11.
6. See CCC, no. 2392.
7. See CCC, nos. 362-365.
8. Congregation for Catholic Education, *Educational Guidance in Human Love* (1983), no. 22f., quoting St. John Paul II, General Audience of January 9, 1980. The latter can be found in St. John Paul II, *Man and Woman He Created Them: A Theology of the Body* (hereafter TOB), trans. Michael Waldstein (Boston: Pauline Books & Media, 2006), no. 14:4. See also USCCB, *United States Catholic Catechism for Adults* (Washington, DC: USCCB, 2006), 412-413.
9. See, for example, TOB, nos. 13-15; *Familiaris Consortio*, no. 37; and St. John Paul II, Encyclical Letter *Veritatis Splendor* (Washington, DC: USCCB, 1993), no. 15. See also Pontifical Council for the Family, *The Truth and Meaning of*

Human Sexuality (1995), no. 10; USCCB, *United States Catholic Catechism for Adults*, 412-413.
10 *Gaudium et Spes*, no. 24; see also TOB, no. 15.
11 See Karol Wojtyła (St. John Paul II), *Love and Responsibility*, trans. H. T. Willets (San Francisco: Ignatius Press, 1993), 28-30.
12 See Pope Benedict XVI, Encyclical Letter *Deus Caritas Est* (Washington, DC: USCCB, 2006), no. 5.
13 Pope Francis, Encyclical Letter *Laudato Si'* (Washington, DC: USCCB, 2015), no. 155.
14 See CCC, nos. 2337-2350.
15 CCC, no. 2337.
16 USCCB, *Catechetical Formation in Chaste Living*, 7.
17 Address during Meeting with Children and Young People, Pastoral Visit to Turin (June 21, 2015).
18 Ibid.
19 See CCC, no. 2351.
20 See CCC, no. 2360.
21 See CCC, nos. 2521-2524. See also Pontifical Council for the Family, *The Truth and Meaning of Human Sexuality*, no. 56.
22 CCC, no. 2342.
23 See CCC, nos. 2360-2379.
24 See Pope Benedict XVI, *Deus Caritas Est*, no. 11.
25 See CCC, nos. 385-421.
26 See CCC, no. 405.
27 CCC, no. 1695.
28 For example, US Code, Title 18, Chapter 110, "Sexual Exploitation and Other Abuse of Children" (sections 2251-2260A). In addition to violating applicable federal or state criminal laws, Catholic clergy may be subject to the canonical delict related to the acquisition, possession or distribution of pornographic images of children under the age of fourteen. See Congregation for the Doctrine of the Faith, *Normae gravioribus delictis* (May 21, 2010), Article 6, §1, 2°.
29 CCC, no. 2354.
30 See CCC, nos. 1854-1864, esp. no. 1860. Also see CCC, no. 2352 on masturbation and the evaluation of the subject's moral responsibility.
31 Authentic art seeks to communicate truth and beauty and lead the viewer to contemplation. When it depicts the human body or a relationship of love, it may include their sexual aspects, but not in an exaggerated way so as to obscure the subject as a whole. Pornography, in contrast, reduces the persons portrayed to their sexual attributes, with the purpose of provoking sensuous craving in the viewer. See Wojtyła, *Love and Responsibility*, 192-193. For

Catholic explanations of art, see CCC, no. 2501; St. John Paul II, *Letter to Artists* (April 4, 1999); and Pope Benedict XVI, Address to Artists (Nov. 21, 2009).

32 See USCCB, *Marriage: Love and Life in the Divine Plan*, 48-49.
33 CCC, no. 2354.
34 See section in Part Four on the victims of pornography, "A Range of Victims," 11.
35 See CCC, nos. 1859, 1874.
36 CCC, no. 1874.
37 See CCC, no. 2352.
38 See Peter C. Kleponis, *Integrity Restored: Helping Catholic Families Win the Battle Against Pornography* (Steubenville, Ohio: Emmaus Road Publishing, 2014), 38-41; and William M. Struthers, *Wired for Intimacy: How Pornography Hijacks the Male Brain* (Downers Grove, IL: IVP Books, 2009), 169-174.
39 See Pope Francis, *Laudato Si'*, esp. no. 123; Address to the European Parliament (Nov. 25, 2014); and Address to a Delegation from the *Dignitatis Humanae* Institute (Dec. 7, 2013).
40 *Gaudium et Spes*, no. 4.
41 See CCC, no. 1869; *Gaudium et Spes*, no. 25; Pontifical Council for Justice and Peace, *Compendium of the Social Doctrine of the Church* (Washington, DC: LEV–USCCB, 2004), no. 119; St. John Paul II, *Sollicitudo Rei Socialis* (December 30, 1987), nos. 36-37; and *Reconciliatio et Paenitentia* (December 2, 1984), no. 16.
42 See Noel J. Bouché, "Exploited: Sex Trafficking, Porn Culture, and the Call to a Lifestyle of Justice," (pureHOPE, 2009); and *Pornography: Driving the Demand in International Sex Trafficking*, ed. David E. Guinn and Julie DiCaro (Los Angeles: Captive Daughters Media, 2007).
43 See USCCB Committee on Migration, *On Human Trafficking* (2007). See also Pope Francis, "Address to Participants in the International Conference on Combating Human Trafficking" (April 20, 2014). The ongoing work of the USCCB Anti-Trafficking Program can be found here: *www.usccb.org/about/anti-trafficking-program/*.
44 Melissa Farley, "Renting an Organ for Ten Minutes: What Tricks Tell Us about Prostitution, Pornography, and Trafficking," in *Pornography: Driving the Demand in International Sex Trafficking*, 144-152.
45 US Department of State, Trafficking Victims Protection Act (2000, and subsequent reauthorizations).
46 Centers for Disease Control and Prevention, webpage "HIV Risk among Adult Sex Workers in the United States" (June 11, 2015): "There is a strong link between sex work and drug and alcohol use"; M. Javanbakht et al.,

"Adult Film Performers: Transmission Behaviors and STI Prevalence," paper presented at the Centers for Disease Control and Prevention STD Prevention Conference (2014); and J. D. Griffith et al., "Pornography Actresses: An Assessment of the Damaged Goods Hypothesis," *The Journal of Sex Research* 50.7 (2013): 621-632.

47 J. Peter and P. M. Valkenburg, "Adolescents' Exposure to a Sexualized Media Environment and Their Notions of Women as Sex Objects," *Sex Roles* 56 (2007): 381-395.

48 Maria Morrow, "Pornography and Penance," in *Leaving and Coming Home: New Wineskins for Catholic Sexual Ethics*, ed. David Cloutier (Eugene, OR: Cascade Books, 2010), 70.

49 See American Psychological Association, "Report of the APA Task Force on the Sexualization of Girls: Executive Summary" (2007, updated 2010).

50 C. Sun, A. Bridges, J. Johnason, and M. Ezzell, "Pornography and the Male Sexual Script: An Analysis of Consumption and Sexual Relations," *Archives of Sexual Behavior* (published online December 2014).

51 Ana Bridges et al., "Aggression and sexual behavior in best-selling pornography videos: A content analysis update," *Violence Against Women* 16 (October 2010): 1065-1085.

52 C. A. Simmons, P. Lehmann, and S. Collier-Tennison, "Linking male use of the sex industry to controlling behavior in violent relationships: An exploratory analysis," *Violence Against Women* 14 (2008): 406-417; and Janet Hinson Shoppe, "When words are not enough: The search for the effect of pornography on abused women," *Violence Against Women* 10 (2004): 56-72.

53 See Barrie Gunter, *Media and the Sexualization of Childhood* (New York: Routledge, 2014).

54 Pamela Paul, *Pornified: How Pornography is Damaging Our Lives, Our Relationships, and Our Families* (New York: Holt Paperbacks, 2005), 163. In an independent poll commissioned by the author and conducted by Harris Interactive, 34% of women and 17% of men equated viewing pornography with cheating. 41% of men and 18% of women said that pornography should never be considered cheating. More recent surveys have confirmed the same trends: ChristianMingle.com and JDate.com, "State of Dating in America" (2014) and *MSNBC.com survey* (2007).

55 Pamela Paul, "From Pornography to Porno to Porn: How Porn Became the Norm," in *The Social Costs of Pornography: A Collection of Papers*, ed. James R. Stoner, Jr. and Donna M. Hughes (Witherspoon Institute: 2010), 3-20, at 8-9.

56 See, for example, Pope Francis's Message for the 48th World Communication Day (June 1, 2014) and Pope Benedict XVI's Message for the 47th World Communications Day (May 12, 2013). See also the Pontifical Council

for Social Communications, *The Church and Internet* and *Ethics in Internet* (February 22, 2002).

57 Studies have shown what is known as the Coolidge Effect, that exposure to new sexual images causes renewed sexual interest, largely due to an increase in the neurotransmitter dopamine. See E. Koukounas and R. Over, "Changes in the magnitude of the eyeblink startle response during habituation of sexual arousal," *Behavior Research and Therapy* 38.6 (2000): 573-584; and Philip Zimbardo and Nikita D. Coulombe, *Man (Dis)connected: How technology has sabotaged what it means to be male* (London: Rider, 2015), 113-114.

58 See Paul M. Barrett, "The new republic of porn," *Bloomberg Businessweek* (June 21, 2012). Exact numbers are impossible to calculate because many pornography companies are privately owned, and there is disagreement about what "counts" as pornography. Further, Barrett reports that between 2007 and 2011, global revenues from pornography may have been reduced by half due to the increased availability of free pornography online.

59 US Code, Title 18, Chapter 71, "Obscenity" (sections 1460-1470); and Chapter 110, "Sexual Exploitation and Other Abuse of Children" (sections 2251-2260A). For an explanation of these laws, and an example of advocacy for more consistent enforcement of them, see the website *http://waronillegalpornography.com/laws/*, a project of the National Center on Sexual Exploitation (formerly Morality in Media).

60 For example, there is the Free Speech Coalition, a trade association of the "adult entertainment" industry in the United States. See the work of the National Center on Sexual Exploitation, which advocates for strong anti-pornography laws.

61 Ana Bridges et al., "Aggression and sexual behavior in best-selling pornography videos."

62 Recent surveys include the *Relationships in America* survey (2014) sponsored by The Austin Institute for the Study of Family and Culture, which found that 43% of men (26% of weekly Church attendees) and 9% of women accessed pornography in the past week; and the *ProvenMen.org Pornography Addiction Survey* (2014) conducted by the Barna Group, which found that 64% of men view pornography monthly (55% of married men), and 29% of young men (18-30) view it daily.

63 According to the Pew Research Center, from 2007 to 2013, the number of women who reported watching "adult videos" grew from 1% to 8%. See Pew Internet & American Life Project, "Online Video" (2007), 18, and Pew Research Center, "Online Video 2013" (2013), 3. The *Relationships in America* survey found that pornography use is more common among younger

women: 19% of women under 30 reported accessing pornography in the past week, compared to 3% of women in their 50s.

64 See *Relationships in America*, 27.
65 Kleponis, *Integrity Restored*, 116, citing "Pornography Statistics," *Family Safe Media* (2010). See also Chiara Sabina et al., "The nature and dynamics of Internet pornography exposure for youth," *Cyberpsychology and Behavior* 11 (2008): 691-693.
66 Struthers, *Wired for Intimacy*, 84-85.
67 J. Brian Bransfield, *Overcoming Pornography Addiction: A Spiritual Solution* (New York: Paulist Press, 2013), 16-20.
68 Viewing pornography has been shown to interfere with short-term memory: C. Laier, F. P. Schulte, and M. Brand, "Pornographic Picture Processing Interferes with Working Memory Performance," *The Journal of Sex Research* 50.7 (2013): 642-652.
69 T. E. Kasper, M. B. Short, and A. C. Milam, "Narcissism and Internet Pornography Use," *Sex & Marital Therapy* 41.5 (2015): 481-486. This study found that the hours spent watching pornography was positively correlated to a higher narcissism level in participants. Narcissism refers to a person's inflated sense of self-importance, a deep need for admiration, and a lack of empathy for others.
70 Regular use of pornography has been shown to correlate with support of marriage redefinition, as well as criticism of marriage in general: Mark Regnerus, "Porn Use and Supporting Same-Sex Marriage," *Public Discourse* (Dec. 20, 2012); and P. J. Wright and A. K. Randall, "Pornography Consumption, Education, and Support for Same-Sex Marriage Among Adult U.S. Males," *Communication Research* 41.5 (July 2014): 665-689.
71 For first-person narratives of women who struggled with pornography use and addiction, and found healing, see *Delivered: True Stories of Men and Women Who Turned from Porn to Purity*, ed. Matt Fradd (San Diego: Catholic Answers Press, 2013).
72 See Kleponis, *Integrity Restored*, 79; Steven E. Rhoads, *Taking Sex Differences Seriously* (San Francisco: Encounter Books, 2004), 51-52; and Ogi Ogasa and Sai Gaddam, *A Billion Wicked Thoughts: What the Internet Tells Us About Sexual Relationships* (New York: Plume, 2011). As a recent example, women constituted 80% of buyers of the *Fifty Shades of Grey* trilogy (Bowker Market Research's *Books & Consumer* monthly survey, November 2012). See also A. Bonomi, et al., "Fiction or Not? Fifty Shades is Associated with Health Risks in Adolescents and Young Adult Females," *Journal of Women's Health* 23.9 (Aug 2014): 720-728, which found that young adult women who read

Fifty Shades of Grey were more likely than non-readers to exhibit signs of eating disorders and have a verbally abusive boyfriend.

73 See Bransfield, *Overcoming Pornography Addiction*, 28-30; and Kleponis, *Integrity Restored*, 33-57.

74 Scientific research on this phenomenon include Valerie Voon, et al., "Neural Correlates of Sexual Cue Reactivity in Individuals with and without Compulsive Sexual Behavior," *PLOS ONE* 9.7 (2014); Simone Kühn and Jürgen Gallinat, "Brain Structure and Functional Connectivity Associated With Pornography Consumption: The Brain on Porn," *JAMA Psychiatry* 71.7 (2014): 827-834; D. L. Hilton, "Pornography addiction—a supranormal stimulus considered in the context of neuroplasticity," *Socioaffective Neuroscience & Psychology* 3 (2013); and D. L. Hilton and C. Watts, "Pornography addiction: a neuroscience perspective," *Surgical Neurology International* 2.19 (2011). See also Struthers, *Wired for Intimacy*, 83-111; and Morgan Bennett, "The New Narcotic," *Public Discourse* (October 9, 2013).

75 See Mark R. Laaser, *Healing the Wounds of Sexual Addiction* (Grand Rapids: Zondervan, 2004).

76 For the link between pornography use and prostitution, see Mary Anne Layden, "Pornography and Violence: A New Look at the Research," *The Social Costs of Pornography*, 57-68, at 66.

77 See note 30 above.

78 By age 5, half of kids go online daily; by age 13, three-quarters of kids have a mobile phone. On average, 15- to 18-year olds spend at least an hour per day consuming media on their phones: Covenant Eyes, "Protecting Your Family Online: A How-To Guide for Parents" (2013). 71% of teens have done something to hide what they do online from their parents: Jamie Le, "The Digital Divide: How the Online Behavior of Teens is Getting Past Parents," *McAfee.com* (June 2012).

79 See note 65 above.

80 Chiara Sabina et al., "The nature and dynamics of Internet pornography exposure for youth"; L. M. Jones, K. J. Mitchell, and D. Filkelhor, "Trends in youth internet victimization: Findings from three youth internet safety surveys 2000-2010," *Journal of Adolescent Health* 50 (2012): 179-186.

81 Christina Coleman, "Some parents angry about graphic sex education book," *USA Today* (May 6, 2014); Veronica Rocha, "Textbook shelved after sex toy, bondage topics spark protest," *LA Times* (August 11, 2014).

82 See Internet Watch Foundation, "Emerging Patterns and Trends Report #1: Youth-Produced Sexual Content" (March 10, 2015); K. Martinez-Prather and D. M. Vandiver, "Sexting among Teenagers in the United

States: A Retrospective Analysis of Identifying Motivating Factors, Potential Targets, and the Role of a Capable Guardian," *International Journal of Cyber Criminology* 8.1 (Jan-June 2014): 21-35; and Amanda Lenhart, "Teens and Sexting," *Pew Research Center* (Dec. 15, 2009). Sexting is also becoming more common among adults over 18: Amanda Lenhart and Maeve Duggan, "Couples, the Internet, and Social Media," *Pew Research Center* (Feb. 11, 2014).

83 Jeff R. Temple, et al., "Teen sexting and its association with sexual behaviors," *Pediatrics and Adolescent Medicine* 166.9 (Sept 2012): 828-833.

84 Justin Jouvenal, "Teen 'sexting' case goes to trial in Fairfax County," *Washington Post* (April 17, 2013); Michelle Miller and Phil Hirschkorn, "'Sexting' Leads to Child Porn Charges for Teens," *CBS News* (June 5, 2010). For legal analysis of this issue, see Mary G. Leary, "Self Produced Child Pornography: The Appropriate Societal Response to Juvenile Self-Sexual Exploitation," *Virginia Journal of Social Policy and the Law* 15.1 (2008).

85 Randi Kaye, "How a cell phone picture led to girl's suicide," *CNN* (October 7, 2010); "Jessica Logan Suicide: Parents of Dead Teen Sue School, Friends Over Sexting Harassment," *Huffington Post* (March 18, 2010).

86 Pornography is also used by perpetrators to make children and youth feel complicit and therefore less likely to report abuse.

87 M. Flood, "The Harms of Pornography Exposure Among Children and Young People," *Child Abuse Review* 18 (2009): 384-400.

88 J. Peter and P. M. Valkenburg, "Adolescents' exposure to a sexualized media environment."

89 Jill Manning, "Hearing on pornography's impact on marriage & the family," US Senate Hearing (November 10, 2005); and M. Flood, "The Harms of Pornography Exposure."

90 Manning, Hearing; and J. Brown and K. L'Engle, "X-Rated: Sexual attitudes and behaviors associated with U.S. early adolescents' exposure to sexually explicit media," *Communication Research* 36 (2009): 129-151.

91 Risky sexual behavior includes having more sex partners and using alcohol or drugs during sexual encounters. D. Braun-Courville and M. Rojas, "Exposure to sexually explicit web sites and adolescent sexual attitudes and behaviors," *Journal of Adolescent Health* 45 (2009): 156-162.

92 Manning, Hearing, citing Robert E. Freeman-Longo, "Children, teens, and sex on the Internet," *Sexual Addiction & Compulsivity* 7 (2000): 75-90.

93 American Psychological Association, "Report of the APA Task Force on the Sexualization of Girls."

94 M. Ybarra et al., "X-rated material and perpetration of sexually aggressive behavior among children and adolescents: is there a link?" *Aggressive Behavior* 37.1 (2011): 1-18; J. Brown and K. L'Engle, "X-Rated"; and S. Bonino, et al., "Use of Pornography and Self-Reported Engagement in Sexual Violence Among Adolescents," *European Journal of Developmental Psychology* 3.3 (2006): 265-288.

95 US Code, Title 18, Chapter 110, "Sexual Exploitation and Other Abuse of Children" (sections 2251-2260A). See also note 28 above.

96 US Department of State, Trafficking Victims Protection Act.

97 For more information about circumstances that make children vulnerable to being used in child pornography, see ECPAT International, "Questions & Answers about the Commercial Sexual Exploitation of Children," 4th edition (2008): 25-29.

98 See USCCB, *Marriage: Love and Life in the Divine Plan*, 48-49.

99 Patrick F. Fagan, "The Effects of Pornography on Individuals, Marriage, Family, and Community," *Marriage and Religion Research Institute* (December 2009); Jonathan Dedmon, "Is the Internet bad for your marriage? Online affairs, pornographic sites playing greater role in divorces," Press Release (2003) re: report from American Academy of Matrimonial Lawyers; and Pamela Paul, "The Porn Factor," *TIME Magazine* (January 19, 2004).

100 Barbara A. Steffens and Robyn L. Rennie, "The traumatic nature of disclosure for wives of sexual addicts," *Sexual Addiction & Compulsivity* 13 (2006); Barbara A. Steffens and Marsha Means, *Your sexually addicted spouse: How partners can cope and heal* (2009); and Kleponis, *Integrity Restored*, 102-110.

101 Paul J. Wright et al., "More than a dalliance? Pornography consumption and extramarital sex attitudes among married U.S. adults," *Psychology of Popular Media Culture* 3.2 (2014): 97-109; and S. Stack, I. Wasserman, and R. Kern, "Adult Social Bonds and Use of Internet Pornography," *Social Science Quarterly* 85 (2004): 75-88.

102 Paul J. Wright et al., "More than a dalliance?"; Ana J. Bridges, "Pornography's Effects on Interpersonal Relationships," in *The Social Costs of Pornography*, 89-110, at 104-106; and Jennifer P. Schneider, "Effects of cybersex addiction on the family: Results of a survey," *Sexual Addiction & Compulsivity* 7 (2000): 34-58. Note that in contrast, one study found that happily married people were 61% less likely to report having viewed pornography in the last thirty days (S. Stack, "Adult Social Bonds").

103 Valerie Voon, et al., "Neural Correlates of Sexual Cue Reactivity": this study, cited above, found greater than average sexual impairment and dysfunction among male compulsive pornography users (average age = 25) in their intimate relationships, although not when using pornographic material. See also

Kleponis, *Integrity Restored*, 66-67; Zimbardo, *Man Dis(connected)*, 107-110; Gary Wilson, *Your Brain on Porn: Internet Pornography and the Emerging Science of Addiction* (UK: Commonwealth, 2014), 27-36; and Gary Wilson, "Why do I find porn more exciting than a partner? Neuroscience reveals how Internet porn can trump real sex," *Psychology Today* (Jan. 17, 2012).

104 C. Sun, et al., "Pornography and the Male Sexual Script"; and Eunjung Ryu, "Spousal Use of Pornography and Its Clinical Significance for Asian-American Women: Korean Women as an Illustration," *Journal of Feminist Family Theory* 16.4 (2004): 75-89.

105 Michael Malcolm and George Naufal, "Are Pornography and Marriage Substitutes for Young Men?" *Institute for the Study of Labor* (November 2014); and Mark Regnerus and Jeremy Uecker, *Premarital Sex in America: How Young Americans Meet, Mate, and Think About Marrying* (Oxford: Oxford University Press, 2011), 93-100.

106 Pornography use has been shown to be correlated with greater acceptance of sex before marriage in general: J. S. Carroll, et al., "Generation XXX: Pornography acceptance and use among emerging adults," *Journal of Adolescent Research* 23.1 (2008): 6-30; and P. J. Wright, "American's attitudes toward premarital sex and pornography consumption: a national panel analysis," *Archive of Sexual Behavior* 44.1 (Jan 2015): 89-97.

107 Pope Francis, Lenten Message for 2014 (December 26, 2013).

108 As quoted in Antonio Spadaro, SJ, "A Big Heart Open to God: The exclusive interview with Pope Francis," *America* (Sept. 30, 2013).

109 See Pope Francis, *Evangelii Gaudium*, no. 3, and Bull of Indiction of the Extraordinary Jubilee of Mercy *Misericordiae Vultus* (April 11, 2015).

110 See USCCB, *When I Call for Help: A Pastoral Response to Domestic Violence* (1992, reissued 2002).

111 In cases where there is a pattern of ongoing, violent abuse, healing a marriage may not be possible. As already stated, it is vital to remove oneself from any danger, to ensure one's safety and the safety of one's children, and to seek appropriate help and support.

112 St. John Paul II, Encyclical Letter *Evangelium Vitae* (Washington, DC: USCCB, 1995), no. 97. See also Pontifical Council for the Family, *The Truth and Meaning of Human Sexuality*.

113 The *Charter* and other information about the Church's work to protect children and young people can be found at *www.usccb.org/issues-and-action/child-and-youth-protection/charter.cfm*.